COURAGEOUS

WARRIORS

COURAGEOUS WARRIORS

Overcoming Obstacles to
Inspire and Lead

Lee F. Satterfield

To order additional copies of this book, contact:
Xlibris
1-888-795-4274
www.Xlibris.com
Orders@Xlibris.com
758462

CONTENTS

ACKNOWLEDGEMENTS

Thank you to Amy Luu for her significant contributions to the manuscript and Jason Colston for his incredible photography skills.

Dedication

To Christopher Canales for the gift of life

PREFACE

In 1988, Sophia was a fifteen-year-old, eleventh-grade, straight-A student with a four-year academic scholarship to a local university. She shared an apartment with her mother, ten-year-old sister, and six-year-old brother. Her mother's boyfriend, Milton Mills, lived with them. On May 20, at approximately 8:30 p.m., Sophia came home from work and saw Mills leaning out of the window. Mills shouted, "Hi, sweetheart!"

Sophia did not expect him to be home because her mother had told Mills to move out that day. When she walked through the front door, she heard loud music and noticed that the TV was also turned up to a high volume. Mills told her that her siblings were visiting a neighbor in the building. He asked her to close her eyes because he had a surprise for her. When she did, he punched her in the mouth. As a result of the unexpected blow, she fell to the floor. She screamed and tried to escape. He knocked her to the floor once again, placing one hand over her mouth and the other on her throat. She continued to scream, and he began hitting her with a pillow and threatened to beat her with a marble ashtray.

Mills ordered her to undress and told her that if she did not do so, he would go to the apartment where her brother and sister were and kill them. Afraid for her siblings, Sophia took off all her clothes. He began to sodomize her and continued to do so repeatedly over the course of the next three hours. Throughout the ordeal, Sophia's mother, who had planned on staying at work until Mills had moved out, called the home and spoke to her several times. Sophia never mentioned what was transpiring out of fear of what would happen to her brother and sister. During one of their phone conversations from her mother's bedroom, Sophia noticed blood on the rug near the closet door. She then saw two bodies and recognized them as those of her siblings.

Mills commanded her to get on the floor and gave her his bathrobe. The phone rang once again, and the caller turned out to be a friend of hers. Mills told Sophia that he was going to the bathroom and that she better be off the phone when he returned. As soon as he left the room, she unlocked the apartment door and fled down the street to a pizzeria, where she told an employee what happened. The police were called. After they discovered the two bodies in the apartment, the police searched for and found Mills and arrested and charged him with first-degree murder, sodomy, and attempted rape.

I met Sophia because I was the prosecutor originally assigned to institute proceedings against Mills. Before the trial, I changed jobs, and the case was handed over to David Schertler, the new prosecutor. He tried the case before a jury, which found Mills guilty of two counts of first-degree murder, two counts of sodomy, and one count of rape. Mills was ultimately sentenced and remains in jail today.

More than twenty-five years later, the detective who had been assigned to Sophia's case brought Sophia to see me in my chambers. Her mother, her twenty-one-year-old daughter, and Schertler joined us. During the reunion, I learned that Sophia was the office manager for the chief administrative judge of Prince George's County Courts. We talked for three hours, recalling the tragedy, the deaths of her siblings, the trial, and most important, all the things that Sophia did to overcome these obstacles in order to get to where she was at the time of our meeting.

As I listened to Sophia and reflected on everything that she had gone through, I became awed by the strength it had taken for her to move on successfully in life. "You are a courageous warrior," I told her.

We live among many courageous warriors, and I have met many of them during my professional career. Another is Patricia "Patty" Broderick. Patty is an associate judge of the Superior Court of the District of Columbia and one of the strongest individuals that I know. Before she became a judge, she was a prosecutor in the same organization where I worked at when I met Sophia. She tried many serious criminal matters, similar to those that she had presided over as a judge. And she did it all in a wheelchair. When she was twenty years old, just before entering her senior year at Trinity College, Patty was in the front passenger seat of a car driven by a friend, an inexperienced driver, who had difficulty navigating a curved road and lost control of the car, which jettisoned across the road into an embankment.

The impact caused the vehicle to flip on its side, trapping Patty inside with her seat belt on. The car did not have any airbags. She immediately felt a sensation race through her body. When her friend asked her if she was all right, Patty responded no and that either her back or neck was broken.

The accident left Patty a paraplegic. She stayed in the hospital for a month and underwent rehabilitation for eight months before she was able to return to her New Jersey home. During rehab, she took two courses at Hofstra College, determined to move forward with a college degree. When she graduated from Trinity College, she realized that a sociology degree in a wheelchair might not get her very far, so she went on to get a degree in rehabilitation counseling at George Washington University in order to work with people in situations similar to hers. The more Patty did, the more she realized what she could do, although with extra effort. She went on to get a law degree from the Columbus School of Law at Catholic University. Afterward, she clerked for a judge at the Superior Court of the District of Columbia. When she applied for a job in the prosecutor's office, she was originally rejected, so she reapplied the next year and was accepted.

President Bill Clinton appointed Patty to the Superior Court in 1998. She has distinguished herself there, earning a reputation for treating litigants, attorneys, and staff with equal respect, and receiving accolades for her handling of both criminal and juvenile cases. I consider her another courageous warrior.

A courageous warrior is someone who has suffered a severe setback but, instead of being overwhelmed, manages to make a comeback. The opposite of a courageous warrior is one who succumbs to their challenges because they are conditioned to fail. The familiar story about the circus elephant comes to mind. The elephant's trainer chained the elephant's foot to a tree surrounded by a fence with an open gate. The chain allowed the elephant to go as far as the gate, but not through it. After being chained to the tree for a period of time, the trainer removed the chain from the elephant's foot but left everything else the same. Instead of going through the open gate, the elephant walked right up to it and stopped. It never went through the gate because it was conditioned to stop in front of it.

Unlike the elephant, courageous warriors use their challenges, failures, and obstacles to propel themselves forward. "People can surmount what seems to be total defeat, difficulties too great to be borne," Eleanor Roosevelt wrote, "but it requires a capacity to readjust endlessly to the changing conditions of life."

I have been a judge for twenty-five years and have been inspired by many people in my courtroom who dealt with difficult challenges—individuals who were victims of child abuse, domestic violence, and sexual abuse; those who lost loved ones to violence; people who have suffered from drug and alcohol addiction—and yet have managed to turn these setbacks into phenomenal comebacks. The best part of being a judge is witnessing how resilient human beings are in meeting life's trials and tribulations.

These stories have been inspirational to me at times when I needed them most, and there have been many such times, for my life has been a story of setbacks and comebacks. I learned way back as a teenager that it was necessary to be able to readjust constantly. With the help of many people (too many to mention), I did. You can too.

I wrote this book—the story of my life—in the hope that reading it will give you the courage, the strength, and the tools to overcome both the ordinary and extraordinary obstacles that you will be confronted with throughout your lifetime.

CHAPTER 1

I had a very normal—some would say privileged—childhood. I was born in 1958 in the District of Columbia and raised in a two-parent household with an older brother, Lawrence, and younger sister, Lori. My father was a lawyer; my mother received her master's degree in childhood education and spent the majority of her professional career in the Department of Recreation, managing day care centers for children of low-income residents. Like many mothers, she was the soul of our family, watching out for everyone and very protective of her children—too protective, we argued sometimes, but she knew that was the case.

I was given my father's first name, Lee, as my first name, and my maternal grandfather's first name, Furman, as my middle name. (The story goes that when Lawrence was born, my mother was not too pleased with my father, and so my brother was not given my father's name, although she allowed him to have my father's middle name.) As a result, I was fortunate to be named after two of the most important men in my life. My grandfather, Furman Herron, was born in the South and later moved to DC, where he met his future wife, Edgenora. He was a good role model to my dad, brother, cousins, and me. He loved his wife dearly, went to church every weekend, and raised his two daughters with love and discipline. In fact, he had a large part in raising all of us.

Lawrence and I attended Catholic schools. He was only fourteen months older, so we did everything together—kickball in the alley, neighborhood parties, sporting events. Lori, who was nine years younger, grew up separately and was raised differently. My brother and I were expected to follow the rules set by our mother, and if we did not, we were disciplined. I followed them the majority of the time—but him? Not so much. Once, when he was acting like a clown, our father told him to pack his bags because he was taking him to the circus. I was scared for my brother until he assured me that he was just attempting to make a point.

Going into my senior year at Saint John's College High School, I was completely preoccupied with one thing: becoming a track star. The previous spring, I had proven that I was one of the fastest runners at my school. By placing second in the 400-meter race at the Catholic High School championship meet, I secured a spot on a local track team, the DC Striders, for the summer. And what a summer it turned out to be! Running in different meets in various cities along the East Coast was thrilling. Spending time with other sprinters, even one who almost ran in the Olympics, added an extra level of excitement. So when school started again in September, I was pretty confident that I would be first in the 400-meter for the fall and spring track seasons—at least, in the Catholic League anyway. Of course, the dream was helped by the fact that the runner who had beaten me in the previous season had graduated.

I had never faced adversity in my life, and it never occurred to me on that beautiful, crisp fall day at the beginning of my senior year that my life was about to be changed forever. I was an athlete preparing for what I hoped would be a victorious spring track season by running in a fall cross-country meet. I had no expectation of winning; long-distance track was not my strength. I was doing all I could to keep up with the other runners because this was my preparation for the future.

As I ran through the wooded area, I felt my left ankle turn and start throbbing. I thought the discomfort was just the pain of training, so I continued to run. Although I did not expect to win, I did expect to finish. As I limped to the finish line, I thought that I had sprained my ankle; the pain was not enough for a broken bone. I had fractured my foot years before at the Boys and Girls Club in Georgetown, and that had been much more painful. I figured an Ace bandage and some ice would take care of it. Secretly, this made me happy because this meant that I would not have to participate in any more cross-country meets. Two weeks passed and there was no improvement. My ankle was still tender, which made it difficult to walk. I finally decided to go to the doctor. An X-ray confirmed what I had thought—no broken bones. I continued to bandage and ice it.

Fall turned to winter, and my ankle was not getting any better. I went back to the doctor for another X-ray. On New Year's Eve, the doctor made a home visit. He and my father went outside and talked for several minutes. When my father came back inside, he spoke with my mother. They later told me that the doctor recommended a biopsy. At that time, I did not know what a biopsy was, much less why it was necessary. Those questions lingered, unanswered, as I sat quietly listening to the doctor and my parents discuss the details of the procedure. One week later, I was at Providence Hospital undergoing the biopsy on my left ankle. After it was done, I was in my hospital bed in tremendous pain, more severe than anything I had ever experienced. At some point, the doctor came into the room with my parents and told me what had been discussed during the home visit was the reason my ankle did not heal. He informed me I had a tumor in my bone, which he believed was cancerous.

Cancer? It did not register. "Osteosarcoma," he said, as though that would explain it. I could not concentrate on the diagnosis. I just wanted to get rid of this awful pain. In fact, the pain was so great that evening that the fact that I had cancer never crossed my mind. I checked out of the hospital the following afternoon and waited for what was next. A few days later, I was at the National Institutes of Health (NIH), a biomedical research facility run by the federal government, to meet with doctors regarding the cancer. Until that day, I had not said much about the diagnosis, and little was made known to me. I was hoping that they could take care of the situation before the spring track season began; I was looking forward to winning the 400-meter dash. My courage to talk about my lofty expectations started to wane as I walked through the pediatric ward and noticed all the kids with bald heads and only one leg. I felt their eyes follow me as I walked down the corridor to an office. Finally, a doctor arrived. He was a young surgeon. "We are going to have to amputate your leg above the left knee," he said matter-of-factly as he took his hand and swiped it across my leg where he would cut.

I stared at that hand. Surely, the surgeon did not know that I was a budding track star with the intention of winning the 400-meter that spring; otherwise, he would have chosen a different form of treatment. Although I had seen the kids in the ward with their leg amputated, it never dawned on me that I was going to be one of them. My parents did not seem surprised by the news. Had they known about this the whole time? I realized what the doctor who performed the biopsy, the kids in the corridor, and the surgeon knew. Talk about being the last to know! I would not be ready for the next track season or any other track season ever again. The only way to describe my reaction was shock—the kind that blurs the mind. I remember my parents speaking to the surgeon in quiet, somber tones, but I could not make out the words. I was numb. The surgeon went on to say that amputation followed by extensive chemotherapy was the course of treatment for the bone cancer. I did not know at the time that when he had told my parents about the treatment, he had said that it would give me the best chance of survival. I never thought that my survival was in question. What healthy seventeen-year-old boy would think that?

My two closest friends were my brother and Kiko, my high school classmate, whom I met in eighth grade. When I asked him about his name and complexion, he explained that his mother was Japanese and his father was African-American. He had taken on the nickname Kiko because no one could pronounce his Japanese name.

Kiko and I joked around a lot, hung out around the city with the girls we met, and just had great fun. However, my cancer made us both older and more serious. Kiko was a starter on the varsity basketball team and, thus, acutely aware of what the amputation would mean for me. My brother was also having a hard time comprehending the fact that I would never be able to run again. Both of them were very worried, but neither of them expressed those feelings to me. It was probably for the best since I found it difficult to be calm about the surgery. What was important was that both of them were supportive, and that was extremely helpful. My brother was upbeat and Kiko was down, but both showed concern in their eyes, sharing my ordeal silently, adopting it as theirs.

After the surgical procedure when I woke up from the anesthesia, there was a cast over what was now a stump of my left leg. On the bright side, I was not in as much pain as I had experienced after the biopsy. They must have better drugs at NIH. The very next day, I was in physical therapy and fitted with a pole connected to a prosthetic foot, which was attached to the cast. I was standing up again. "The sooner, the better," my therapist said. A week later, I was back home with a temporary leg, cane, and crutches.

I did not understand the expression sick as a dog until I received my first chemotherapy treatment. After the surgeon had told me about amputating my leg at NIH, he also talked about chemotherapy treatments. I was preoccupied at the time and did not hear what chemotherapy was or what the side effects might be. In his matter-of-fact manner once again, he explained that I would probably experience nausea and certainly hair loss. Hair loss? He could not be talking about the hair on my head because losing a leg was bad enough. Here I was, a senior in high school, with one leg and soon no hair, and the senior prom was just a few months away. This could not be happening to me. Would I get a date to the prom? Did I want to go to it anyway? How could you dance with one leg? Kojak was a popular TV show at the time, but whereas the bald-headed look on the show's star, Telly Savalas, had become popular, I did not think it would go over as well on a high school senior.

My family helped to ease my way through the chemo. My grandfather was ever present. He took me to doctor appointments, sat with me while I underwent treatment, and maintained a positive attitude. There was never a time where I saw him discouraged because of my circumstances. I adored him. When I lost my hair, I saw it as an opportunity to look like him. He frequently dressed in blue denim overalls, so I purchased a pair. We would go to my treatments, both with our heads bald, dressed identically. I knew I had accomplished my goal when a nurse commented that we looked like father and son.

Just like the surgeon had predicted, the monthly chemo made me ill each time. As the treatment continued, I would start to vomit before the medicine was even hooked up to me intravenously. Luckily, nurse Krueger, whose son attended my school, came to my rescue. She checked on me even when she was not assigned to do so during my earlier treatments.

Everyone at the high school was very supportive. It was a military school with mandatory Reserve Officers' Training Corps. I was lieutenant colonel in charge of the regimental marching band and a trumpet player. During my first several weeks in chemo, I had a tutor and was able to keep up with my assignments. Graduating on time with my class was important to me; not doing so was not an option. Except for the treatments, things seemed to be getting more normal as the months went by.

The marching band went on a trip every year, and the trip that year was to London. I wanted very much to go, to prove that I could handle it, even with just one leg. It was an affirmation for me, a sign that I could continue my normal life. On the other hand, my parents were less enthusiastic about it due to the possibility that getting around might be difficult. However, this was something we had all looked forward to for quite some time, and I think my parents must have sensed this. At the same time, they worried about how I would do because they gave me permission to go, but my father announced that he was going as well, as a chaperone. Not only that, nurse Krueger, whose son was a trombone player in the band, was also tagging along. I had a sinking suspicion that some negotiations had been going on behind my back, but it was one of those things I never asked because I did not want to know. I preferred to believe that they had each wanted to see London and hear the band play. And play we did at several London venues. I enjoyed playing my trumpet, but did not have that great of a time because I was not as mobile as my bandmates. I was becoming more aware of how the loss of my leg was going to influence my life. Sensing my depressed state and anxious to cheer me up, my father took me to a tailor, who made me a customized brown suit, which did raise my spirits a little.

When we returned, I kept my eye on the goal I had set. If I remained on pace with the students in my class, it would lessen the blow of losing my leg. I was not going to let this cancer defeat me. This was the beginning of my understanding of how stating my intentions clearly could impact the end result, how envisioning a positive outcome during a setback would give me a better chance of a comeback. That did not mean I wasn't scared from time to time, but I worked hard on maintaining a positive attitude, telling myself that doing so was healthy. This worked for the remainder of my senior year. I was going to graduate with my class, play my trumpet with the quartet at graduation, and prepare for college. Although receiving a track scholarship from Brandeis University was no longer a possibility, they remained interested in me academically. My grades were pretty good, so where my legs could not take me, my mind would.

I attended my senior prom with my girlfriend (someone whom I had known since elementary school and a sweetheart for taking me on during this difficult period in my life), Kiko, and his girlfriend. On the day of the prom, Kiko and I went out on a dry run of the evening by going to the location of the dinner and dance. We wanted to appear cool and in charge but almost did not get the opportunity. As I was driving, we came to a red light, but the car would not stop as I pumped the brakes. My prosthetic foot was stuck underneath it! Luckily, I figured it out in time and did not hit the car in front of me.

The prom was a blast. I danced as well as I could, and the unchaperoned after-party was even better. With the prom, the question about whether I could dance was behind me, and I was beginning to feel as if living with one leg was an obstacle, but not the end of the world. But just when things seemed to be somewhat normal, the doctors noticed a problem during a routine X-ray of my lungs. I had a different doctor who was my treating physician at this point, and she was direct about what was happening to me. "Metastasis to bilateral lungs," she said. The cancer had spread to both lungs.

How could that be? After weeks of chemotherapy, getting sick from the side effects, and hair loss, I now discover that I have cancer in not only one lung but two? Graduation was three weeks away, and college at Brandeis awaited me in the fall. Lung cancer sounded even more serious than bone cancer. If bone cancer did not grab my attention before, lung cancer did now. The doctors already took away my leg, and now they were planning to take my lungs too? Even though I was not always realistic about how seriously ill I was, I knew that there was no life without lungs.

Surgery was the chosen method of treatment, followed by more chemotherapy. I had heard that protocol before. The surgeon explained that he was going to remove a quarter-sized slice from my left lung, and then see if the cancer cells in the right lung would weaken with additional chemotherapy. Once again, I was confined to a hospital bed, this time trying to prepare for final exams. After I was discharged, the chemo continued. I was still going to graduate, but there was some question as to whether I could play my trumpet at graduation. I remember the expression of concern on my parents' faces as I left to practice with the quartet at school. Shortly after, Lawrence entered the room where we were practicing. I was certain I knew why he came; it had to be to stop me from rehearsing. I thought there was about to be a scene, but instead, he said that he wanted me to know that our father had called the doctor, who had cleared me to play.

Graduation was held at the Basilica of the National Shrine of the Immaculate Conception. Before the ceremony ended, the school president surprised me by giving me an award for inspiration. To my surprise, I received a standing ovation. My parents and friends seemed so proud of me. It felt wonderful. Afterward, I rushed to the balcony where the quartet had gathered to play the processional song at the close of graduation, but the award and spontaneous ovation made me too late. As I reached the balcony, I saw our musical director playing the last song of my high school musical career on my trumpet. He knew about the surprise award and had prepared in case there was a delay in my return since he also knew I would be walking, not running back.

The summer before college was normal except for the phantom pains I kept enduring in the leg that was no longer there. I hung out a lot with my girlfriend. She did not seem to mind the Kojak look. I purchased a wig at the advice of the kids in the cancer ward. Many of them were wearing them. However, wigs in 1976 were not as refined as they are today, and for males, the thought of wearing one was a thought worth ditching.

This was my first summer as an amputee. I was wearing my permanent prosthetic leg, and for some reason, the color of it was white, which did not match the color of my skin. It did not matter at that time since I had no intention of wearing shorts or showing it off anyway. Whenever it was very hot or rainy, I experienced severe phantom pains. My doctor explained that it would feel as if my left foot was still attached to my stump, but I did not realize that the sensation would sometimes hurt and frequently keep me awake at night.

In August, my doctor decided it was time to operate on my right lung and remove the remaining cancer. The chemo had not killed off those cells, so surgery was the only solution. By this point, I knew the routine. Be at the hospital the day before surgery. No food after a certain hour. An X-ray shortly before so the surgeon could pinpoint exactly where to operate. Once the procedure was completed, recovery involved a hefty dose of morphine to deaden the pain and the worst part—removing the tubes that were inserted between the lungs to prevent deflation. It felt like a snake was slithering through my chest and out the hole on my side. There was nothing atypical about this surgery, although I always thought that this surgeon must have had bigger hands than the surgeon who operated on my left lung because the incision on my right side was three times the size of the one on my left. I guess he wanted a better view. The operation was followed by more chemo, and at the end of the summer, off to college I went.

Lee with Lawrence and their mother, Lorena Satterfield,
at Lawrence's high school graduation in 1975

National Honor Society Award Ceremony in
1976. Lee is second from the right.

CHAPTER 2

Ironically, a runner who was a year older from a rival high school had recruited me to attend Brandeis University. He was on a mission to bring some of the fastest high school runners from DC to join him at the university. I was accepted, even though I was no longer one of the fastest runners, or a runner at all for that matter. Nonetheless, I was very happy to be at the Waltham, Massachusetts, campus. It was a beautiful place, small enough to get around easily; its paths were lined with trees and bushes. Classes were what I expected—difficult at times but interesting.

John, my roommate, was a good friend from high school who had just lost his mother to cancer the previous year. I felt sorry for him because his parents were divorced, and he and his brother had to go live with their father. In retrospect, you would think that we might have confided in each other about the trauma of cancer and loss, but like most eighteen year old males, we were more comfortable talking about practical things, avoiding all emotional areas. We had only been on campus a few days when the two of us were walking up a hill from a college event and suddenly found ourselves surrounded by a group of white students. "Are you a militant?" one of them asked me. I was sure he wondered why anyone our age other than a militant would choose to be bald, so I ignored him and started to walk away, preferring not to get into the why of my grooming. John, however, did not. He wanted to fight the guy for what he thought was an ignorant comment, but I prevailed, and we both left. The next day, the same guy approached me in the cafeteria and apologized. Evidently, someone had clarified my situation to him. "I didn't realize you have cancer," he explained sympathetically.

The interesting thing about this encounter was that I had no problem being identified as a militant. I thought it was kind of flattering, given that Angela Davis and Abbie Hoffman had attended Brandeis, which was known for being somewhat progressive. Since I no longer had an identity of a budding track star, militant would do. To my chagrin, his comment made me feel that instead of being cool, I was going to be seen as someone with a disability, which of course I was.

There was a lighter side to the disability as well. In an attempt to alleviate pressure around exam time, John and I turned the lights off in the dorm hallway and hung my prosthetic leg from the ceiling. When the students walked by our room to get to the light switch, we flashed our desk lamps on the leg. No matter how often we did it, it scared them every time. I think it helped others feel more comfortable around me. If I could laugh, they could laugh too.

I took a reduced course load because I had to fly back to NIH each month for chemo. My plan was to enroll in summer classes at a university back home so that I would amass enough credits to graduate on time with the class of 1980. Although going back and forth to DC became routine, I soon dreaded it. I felt that I was missing out on campus life, and after all the chemo that I had endured, I knew full well what was in store for me.

Despite all the interruptions, first semester was going well. I began to write poetry or as I called it, lyrics to songs. It was very therapeutic. Since I was unable to talk about my feelings, I needed some sort of emotional outlet. As I put words down on paper, I fantasized that I would become a songwriter one day. It was not as cool as being a militant, but it was definitely better than being a cancer patient.

When I was feeling philosophical about the state of the world, I wrote the poem, "Let's Do It Together, People":

> People, oh people, why don't they love like they used to do?
> Why do they fight one another and break down their brothers?
> Why do they live like they do?
> Let's do it together, people;
> Let's not do it apart from each other.
> Let's do it together, people.
> Let's show the love between one another.

When I felt the pressures of life, I explored that as well:

> I get up and look at my life.
> There is so much pressure involved.
> I feel like I'm going to jump and just run.

Sometimes I feel so afraid that something is going to happen the next day.

It makes me want to deflate all the pressure in my life.

Pressure is a powerful thing.

It builds up on you like a rare disease.

It's as lethal as a strange disease; it will put you away with ease.

At the end of first semester, I was in the hospital for my monthly dose of chemo when the doctor came into my room. "The latest X-ray showed a mass on your lung," she told me, "and with your history, it's likely cancerous."

I felt very much alone. "What are we going to do?" I asked her.

"The surgeon will explain," she responded, and then she left. For the first time since being sick, I was scared that I was never going to get better. The surgeon came in and told me the cancer had spread to my left lung and that they were going to surgically remove the mass just like they had done before. The thought of having to be operated on again inspired me to write "Going Back":

Going back again, seems like it never ends.

Going back to a place, where a change in my life began.

Now I sure don't know the end.

Going to do it all once more, I'm sure to get real sore.

I care but that is my fare.

Going back, when will it end?

I'll try; I'll try to do it once again.

Going back, yes, I really care; I know that God cares for me too.

Going to the same old place, doing it the same old way.

Hey, I say, I'm ready to go right through it again.

Going back to the place, where it's sure to end.

Don't feel sad, I plan to win.

I'm sure it just wouldn't be, without my many friends, thank you.

Thank you, friends, for being with me.

A month later, I was back at NIH for surgery, going through the same drill as the other two times. I worried that the cancer would never go away, but I could not dwell on it. I had to find a way to get to the light at the end of the tunnel: state my intention, set my goal, and hope for the best.

Nevertheless, I was worried. I was not the only one. The doctors were also concerned and decided that a different protocol of treatment was necessary. They intended to zap the cancer cells in my system with all the poison that my body could handle without killing me. To ensure that I would not die as a result, the plan was to take some of my healthy bone marrow and feed it back to me intravenously after the full assault of chemo. In order to avoid any infections, such as pneumonia, I would remain in a sterilized room for three weeks, after which I would continue on one of the drugs I was taking prior to my third occurrence of cancer in the lungs.

This was my life during the first part of second semester. They zapped me pretty well, and for three weeks, I was again sick as a dog. I remember feeling very sorry for myself, but things could have been worse. There was a little girl in the ward losing her battle to cancer. After witnessing her struggles and worrying about my own, I felt that I needed some extra help, so I wrote "Faith":

> I am going to make it to the next day; things are going to go the right way.
> And if you ask me if I pray, I'll tell you, God is my way.
> I think his love is what I need to keep me being me.
> He gives me love that I need from the people that I see.
> You gotta have faith in the man; just consider him a friend.
> If faith is what you need, try to find it just like me.
> I am going to make it to the next day; things are going to go my way.
> So just ask me how you may, and I'll tell you God should be your way.
> Don't forget the man afar 'cause he makes you what you are.
> I wish everyone could see the love he gives to me.
> You gotta have faith in the man; just consider him a friend.
> If faith is what you need, try to find it just like me.
> I am going to make it to the next day; things are going to go the right way.
> And if you ask me if I pray, I'll tell you God is my way.

When I returned to Brandeis, I discovered that the side effects were worse this time around. Painful, bloody blisters formed in my mouth. I used ice to reduce the pain and towels to slow down the bleeding, but it had gotten so bad that I had to fly home several times between my monthly chemo appointments to treat them. I felt awful on the plane, certain that other passengers were staring at me.

My parents remained positive throughout the entire ordeal. I always knew they were there for me. If my condition had them worried, they did not show it. I never saw them cry, curse the situation, or take it out on each other or anyone else for that matter. They refused to show fear and only talked about how we were going to do whatever was necessary so that I could get better. They were certainly tested during this period, because in the midst of my treatments, another incident happened. While running from a store to catch a bus in Boston, Lawrence somehow managed to run straight through a plated, glass window and was seriously injured. I received the news from my dorm manager, and because my brother was attending Boston University nearby, I was the first family member to arrive at the hospital after his accident. He was an ugly sight to look at. His face and leg had been completely sliced up. My parents arrived later that night from DC, and the vigil began. We learned that he would need facial plastic surgery, and that he had temporarily lost all sensation below his left knee. It would take him about a month to recover. After a week, my father returned home to go back to work and take care of Lori. My aunt came to stay with my mother, who remained at a nearby hotel. I got a rental car so that I could travel back and forth from Waltham to Boston to check up on my brother and transport my mother to and from the hospital.

After the accident with Lawrence and continued side effects of the new chemo regime, I became very discouraged. I was fed up with the monthly flights to get cancer-free. When I came home after my second semester, I decided to continue my studies locally in order to keep up with the treatment. I enrolled at the University of Maryland for the fall semester. I regretted not being able to complete college away from home. However, I did not abandon my goal of graduating with the class of 1980; it was just going to be with a different class of 1980.

I began outpatient chemo treatments during the summer. What a disaster! I would go to the hospital on Friday mornings and return home that evening. By nighttime, I was sick, but at least, it happened in the comfort of my own home and not in a bleak hospital room. On one of those nights, my girlfriend broke up with me. Here I was sick with nausea and incapacitated in bed when I received a phone call from her saying that it was time for us to move on. Things had not been that great between us, but I had attended her senior prom and spent most of the summer with her. Now it was suddenly time for her to move on to new adventures.

Then there was a bigger, more serious letdown. During a standard X-ray in early fall, the doctors saw another spot on my lung, which they believed to be malignant. After I had lost my leg, gone through countless months of horrific chemo, and underwent three lung surgeries, they were telling me that they had to operate again. I was more depressed than I had ever been. I was nearing the end of treatment and the cancer had returned! This was the first time where I was not sure I had the energy to continue the fight. What treatment would be next? Would the cancer ever stop coming back? These questions weighed heavily on my mind. I could see the concern on my parents' faces no matter how brave they tried to be. We were just so tired of it all. As much as I wanted to quit, it was not possible to do so. The choices are few in these situations, so you try as best you can to move forward. I had been through this before and told myself that I simply had to do it again.

The night before the surgery, my parents dropped me off at the hospital as usual. They were planning to return sometime toward the end of the operation so they could be there when I gained consciousness. By now, I was nineteen years old and a professional at this, so there was no need for them to be present beforehand. The morning of the operation, I took it as a positive sign that nurse Krueger was on duty. Once again, she was there for me at a time when I needed support.

Before each operation, the surgeon would take a final X-ray of the area to make sure he knew the precise location of the cancerous area. What took place next is why I think that miracles do happen. I was completely shocked when the surgeon came into the room and informed me that he did not see the cancerous spot on my lung in the preparatory X-ray. What the doctors had seen in the previous ones was no longer there! I wondered whether he knew what he was talking about. He assured me that he did and told me to get dressed and go home. Needless to say, I was thrilled, but a little skeptical. "Are they sure?" I asked nurse Krueger.

"Absolutely sure!" she reassured me. "I have an idea! Instead of calling your parents to tell them, how about if I drive you home to surprise them? A little happy surprise never hurt anyone."

So we got into her car and drove to my house. My parents were ecstatic when they heard the good news.

CHAPTER 3

What do Beethoven, Stephen Hawking, Helen Keller, and Franklin D. Roosevelt have in common? They are all highly accomplished and have contributed significantly to society. They also managed to achieve great things while coping with their disabilities. Dr. Martin Luther King Jr. said, "The ultimate measure of a man is not where he stands in moments of comfort and convenience, but where he stands at times of challenges and controversy." All those individuals embody the type of person King talked about—they did not let the discouraging aspects of their disability defeat them.

Disability is defined by Webster as "a physical, mental, cognitive, or developmental condition that impairs, interferes with, or limits a person's ability to engage in certain tasks or actions." By definition, I was a person with a disability. I was an amputee who became limited in physical activities. I had to decide if I was going to be a victim of my circumstances. Was I going to view the world as burdensome or unjust? Or was I going to manage my physical limitation in a positive, productive way?

I chose to not be a victim.

Being active about that choice came gradually. I was a true warrior during my senior year of high school and freshman year of college, battling a deadly disease with everything I had, perfectly willing to give up my leg if it meant victory. However, fighting for your life is different from learning to live with the aftermath. After I had won the battle, I found myself dealing with the fact that my life was never going to be normal again. I felt self-conscious around girls and had trouble keeping up with my friends. During a trip to the beach, I recall needing my prosthetic leg to get to the water's edge, but I could not get into the water with it. When we went to a haunted house, I was not able to run like the others. I felt left behind, a kind of loneliness I had never experienced before. Wearing the prosthetic made me constantly bruised, and when the weather became hot and humid in the summer months, the sweat caused me to slip out of the leg, further humiliating me. In addition to physical obstacles, I perceived myself the way I thought others perceived me, which took an emotional toll. I did not have the courage to wear shorts and expose my prosthetic to public scrutiny until I saw Senator Edward Kennedy's son, who was also a leg amputee, wear shorts on national television. My depression lasted throughout my three years at the University of Maryland. I did not enjoy college. I attended classes, turned in my assignments, and graduated on time, but I felt isolated living at home. I was missing out on all the fun of living on a college campus. I did not have any girlfriends, go to any football games, or attend any parties.

During my junior year, I was appointed by the chancellor to the University Student Appellate Board, and its members elected me as chief judge on my senior year. I majored in economics and minored in English, but enrolled in criminal justice courses for fun. Given that my father was a major influence in my life, it was natural to think of law school as a potential next step.

My father, Lee Arthur Satterfield, was born on September 6, 1933, in Edenton, North Carolina, a town on Albemarle Sound. My father's father abandoned him when he was at an early age. He was raised by a single mother with the help of his mother's younger brother. Although they were so poor that he did not have proper shoes to wear to school, he could easily outrun the other kids barefoot. When he and his mother moved to DC, his running abilities got him the quarterback position on the Cardozo Senior High School football team. While attending high school, he met his future bride, Lorena Herron, who was attending Dunbar Senior High School. After high school, he was drafted into the army during the Korean War. Upon his return, he received his undergraduate and law degrees from Howard University, student finishing them one year faster than usual. My brother and I were born when he was in law school, so my father attended classes during the day and worked to make ends meet as a security guard at night.

My father rose through the legal ranks of the Internal Revenue Service and US Department of Justice to eventually serve as General Counsel at the Chesapeake and Potomac Telephone Company. Even though he spent long hours at the office advancing his professional career, he was still an active parent. He regularly took us to Washington Redskins games. When they made it to Super Bowl XXII in San Diego, Doug Williams was not just the starting quarterback, but also the first African American quarterback to play in the championship game. This fact alone impelled my father and me to get tickets. We flew to Los Angeles, because every hotel in San Diego was booked solid, and drove to San Diego on the morning of the game. When the Denver Broncos had a 10–0 lead, I turned to my father and said, "We came all the way from DC to watch a blowout!"

Everything changed in the second quarter. The Redskins scored five straight touchdowns, and when the game ended, we had witnessed together the first African American quarterback to win a Super Bowl. The song "(I've Had) The Time of My Life" was played over the stadium speakers, and indeed, we were having the time of our lives! We drove back to Los Angeles and spent the entire next day reading newspaper articles about the game and watching highlights.

Not only was he a fun parent, he was a devoted one. He had always wanted to be a judge, and he was in the running to be an associate judge of the DC Superior Court. When I was diagnosed with cancer, he backed out of contention to care for me. He felt that he needed the flexibility to help the family through dark times. My father loved being a lawyer, and I adored him. Since Lawrence took a different path, I applied to the George Washington University Law School. I felt that one of us should follow in my father's footsteps.

CHAPTER 4

Law school kept me busy, and my handicap made me insecure. As a result, I dated very little and did not have any steady girlfriends. One evening during my third year of law school, I went to a club with some friends. An attractive girl caught my eye, and I asked her to dance. Her name was Michelle. We danced together for a couple of songs, and then I asked for her number. Just like that, I had embarked on my first relationship in almost seven years. We dated during the remainder of law school and married after my one-year judicial clerkship with Judge Paul Webber at the Superior Court of the District of Columbia. Neither of us gave it much thought. Marriage seemed like the natural thing to do once you finished school and dated someone for a long time.

Michelle was a preacher's daughter. For that reason, she was intent on receiving marriage counseling through our pastor prior to the union. Over the course of several weeks, he had us perform a number of tasks individually, including answering questions regarding the other party. One of those questions was whether we were attracted to each other. I said yes, but unbeknownst to me, she expressed some reservations because of my physical appearance.

My yes was not entirely truthful. The fact was that I was much more attracted to another woman that I thought I might be in love with. She was a law student serving as a judicial intern that I met during my clerkship several months before. While I was telling the pastor one thing, I was doing another. As we approached our wedding date, I was being unfaithful to my fiancée. If either of us had been aware of the other's feelings at that time, we certainly might have rethought the whole marriage thing. I was not passionately in love and nor was Michelle, but we were headed to the altar and neither of us was brave enough to end it. So we took our vows. After the wedding, I joined the United States Attorney's Office as a prosecutor. I was nervous before my first trial, but was confident in my skills. I was still self-conscious of my appearance though.

My initial cases were misdemeanors involving possession of controlled substances and petty theft. During one of those cases, a journalist was seated as one of the jurors. It was a case with little fanfare. After it was over, the journalist wrote about his experience. In his article, he described me as a gangly youth imploring the jury to convict the accused for simple possession of drugs. I did not know what he meant by gangly, so I looked it up in Webster's Dictionary and discovered that it meant "tall, ungracefully thin, lanky, loose, and awkwardly built." That description was tough to take. Even if I had not been an amputee with a prosthetic, it still would have been tough. I knew all too well that I walked awkwardly due to my disability, and I was upset at how others perceived me. It did not take much to heighten my insecurities about my physical appearance. I wanted to contact the journalist to let him know that I walked with an artificial leg, hoping that would make him feel badly, but I thought better of it. I told myself as I calmed down that I had won the case, which was all that mattered. Besides, amputee or not, I still qualified as gangly.

My second experience was more upsetting than the first one. I appeared in front of a judge who eventually became one of my colleagues. During the hearing, I was having problems communicating via telephone with another prosecutor regarding whether our witnesses for the trial were available in the designated witness room. The judge became so frustrated with the pace of obtaining information that he instructed me to run or limp down to the witness room to figure it out. For a split second, I was so stunned that I refused to believe that a judge would comment in such a manner on my disability. When I saw how upset my colleague, a fellow prosecutor, was about the judge's comment upon my return to the courtroom, I realized that I had heard him correctly. My colleague insisted that we report it to a supervisor, who informed Chief Judge H. Carl Moultrie I. From what I remember, he did nothing about it.

The two incidents were instructive. I learned that I needed to be stronger mentally about my disability and less self-conscious about my outward appearance. Every morning, I was reminded of my missing leg, but I had to leave the reminder at home and get on with my day.

I loved my work as a prosecutor. Several of the cases I handled received media attention. One involved the shooting of an undercover police officer, Troy Pumphrey, a father of two toddlers. Pumphrey was masquerading as a drug dealer and offering the buyers, and subsequently, the defendants, a gallon of PCP. The sale went badly because the defendants did not have the money, so they decided to rob the purported drug dealer of the PCP. They met beforehand and decided that one of them would distract the dealer by discussing the purchase and another would shoot him. Once they had the PCP in their possession, they would flee in a getaway car waiting nearby.

As two police surveillance cars watched on December 16, 1987, the gunman emerged from the darkness behind Pumphrey and shot him once in the back. After he fell to the ground, the driver of the getaway car raced off, leaving his co-conspirators behind. Seeing their partner down, one surveillance team drove toward Pumphrey. The cop in the passenger seat began shooting at the assailants from within the vehicle and ended up accidentally shooting himself in the foot. The officers threw Pumphrey in the car and drove him to a hospital. The so-called buyer was apprehended by the other surveillance team as the gunman fled on foot.

During the trial, I called the police witnesses first, starting with Pumphrey. He could identify the defendant with whom he had arranged the transaction, but not the shooter or driver of the getaway car. The officers in the second surveillance car could not identify any of the assailants, but noted which direction the shooter ran.

There were four suspects, one of whom was seventeen years old. His father was a corrections officer, and the case opened up when his father brought the juvenile into the police station within weeks of the shooting. He was a good kid, but had become caught up with the wrong crowd. I could tell he that would not testify without a protective ploy. He needed to appear to be forced to testify. He was afraid of retribution by the other assailants or their family members; snitching could mean death. At my request, the judge jailed the juvenile for his refusal. In the end, his testimony led to the identification and arrest of the other three suspects and established their conspiracy to steal from the undercover cop.

Before the trial, the grand jury rendered an indictment for conspiracy to commit robbery while armed, assault with the intent to commit robbery while armed, and possession of a firearm during the commission of a crime of violence. As I was preparing the case, I got a huge break. A resident at Bolling Air Force Base had called the military police the night of the shooting to report an intruder near their home. They in turn notified the Metropolitan Police Department, who searched the area and recovered the weapon that had been used to shoot Pumphrey, a .357 Magnum. After the conclusion of the trial, the jury found the three adult defendants guilty on all counts, and they received significant jail time. Although he initially refused, the juvenile was not prosecuted since he testified truthfully.

Another high-profile case involved three students who attended Frank W. Ballou Senior High School. Kendall Merriweather, a seventeen-year-old junior, was walking to school around 10:00 a.m. on December 11,

1987, carrying his books and a boom box given to him by his parents for his birthday. On the way, he stopped by a McDonald's for a snack. After he was finished, he continued walking when he passed by a group of teenagers, including Jared Allen and Rodney Prophet. After Allen and Prophet followed him for three blocks, Allen approached him and demanded the boom box. When Merriweather turned to walk away, Allen pulled out a gun and shot him once in the back. Merriweather fell, and Prophet picked up the boom box and walked down an alley with Allen. The police arrived quickly and were told the direction that the assailants headed. Merriweather's younger brother, who happened to also be around the McDonald's earlier, was able to name them. They tracked them down to an apartment building where Allen and Prophet were found in a hallway playing the boom box.

During the grand jury investigation, I subpoenaed the group of teenagers to testify, but because they were minors, I asked the police to send for their parents. In my experience with juveniles, I found that it could be difficult persuading them to talk, so I wanted to see the parents first and stress to them the importance of their children's cooperation. I left the parents to talk to their children and interviewed them afterward. Their testimonies resulted in Allen and Prophet being convicted of felony murder while armed.

A few years into the marriage, Michelle and I decided that we were ready to start a family. We tried to conceive for a while before we realized that we had a problem. After going to the doctor, it turned out I was the problem. I had no viable semen. At least, that was what Michelle told me over the phone in frustration when she found out the results. She was pretty upset, and I was baffled because I had never imagined that I would have difficulty having a child. A second opinion confirmed the results.

As it turned out, the reason I was alive was also the reason for my infertility. I was still going to NIH for regular precautionary checkups due to my history of cancer. During one of my visits, one of the nurses asked me if I was married. She also asked if I had children to which I responded no. Then she laid the bombshell—it was not uncommon for a cancer patient who received the amount of chemotherapy that I had received to have trouble conceiving. Chemo that is designed to kill bad cells can often kill good ones too. Why didn't someone tell me this before giving me the medicine? I could have stored away a few sperm cells before treatment. How could I blame them though; I was still here on this earth because of the chemo and the NIH doctors.

Strong marriages survive challenges; weak marriages do not. The way we dealt with infertility was a symptom of a poor marriage. There were others, such as a lack of commitment to each other. To deal with our marital woes, I buried myself in my work. Our problems festered, and I devoted even less time to our relationship. We separated after four years of marriage. I learned a lot about myself throughout this period. Differentiating my identity from the marriage led to depression and anger. However, I realized that we were both to blame for our demise.

After the divorce was finalized two years later, I left the attorney's office and joined the law firm of Sachs, Greenebaum and Taylor. I also sold the house that I shared with Michelle so I could purchase another one. I was ready for a fresh start.

Lee with best friend Kiko Washington.

CHAPTER 5

One evening, Pamela, a lovely young lawyer with blond hair, sparkling green eyes, and a vivacious personality, came to my law firm to discuss becoming a prosecutor. A mutual friend had referred her to me. At that time, she was clerking for Judge Nan Huhn, who had presided over my first criminal trial. When I saw how attractive she was, I told her that I was in the midst of preparing for a trial, but happy to take a short break. I suggested that we go out to dinner near my office to talk. Pam was caught off guard since she had planned on a meeting rather than a date, but she went along with it anyway. We chose the same item on the menu, which I viewed as a sign. However, she suggested that we try different dishes, so I ordered something else. She offered me a bite of her dish when the food arrived, but I declined. When I reciprocated the offer, she accepted, which seemed pleasantly intimate. We chatted about her career path, how tough Judge Huhn was, and ourselves.

About a week later, I received a handwritten letter on pink stationary thanking me for the meeting and ending with, "Hope to see you around." I took that last sentence as an invitation to ask her out for a date. Although it was not her intent, she still agreed to it. Our first date was brunch at a Georgetown restaurant, and the conversation flowed so freely that we did not finish until 4:00 p.m. Even though it was a Sunday, Pam had to work, so I dropped her off at the courthouse, which I knew all too well from my prosecutor days. We went on many dates, but one was extraordinary. The police often allowed prosecutors to ride along with them so they could become familiar with their work. To impress Pam, I thought it would be a great idea since she yearned to be a prosecutor. As a favor, one of the homicide detectives I knew arranged one for us.

The beginning of the evening was humdrum, so we went to a pizzeria with the officers to grab some food. While we were there, a call came in about a shooting. We arrived at an apartment complex with sirens blaring. It turned out to be a triple homicide. Surprisingly, the homicide detectives allowed us to accompany them to the scene of the crime. It was eerily calm and quiet. We expected to see blood splattered everywhere, but there was very little; however, the deceased was lying there with 9mm-bullet holes. Because this was going to be an all-nighter for the detectives, they put us in another police car to take us back to mine.

When I took her home, I told Pam that I was still technically married, but that the divorce papers were filed. Despite the morbidity of the night, I kissed her for the first time. The next day, she said that she had not slept well the night before. I wondered whether it was because she had witnessed a murder scene, or that I was still attached to someone else. This marked the beginning of more traditional dates, such as attending shows, going to the movies, and trying out new restaurants. It was not long before my bachelor pad was closed off to all Washington's single women but Pam.

We had our first argument canoeing on the Potomac River. I wanted to stay on the calm canal; she wanted to try rougher waters. I gave in, but it turned out to be tougher than either of us had anticipated, and we got a little heated with each other. Once we made it safely back to shore, we calmed down after eating the sandwiches that she had made. We went back to my place and made up.

I completely fell for this woman. She was attractive, energetic, intelligent, and a lot of fun. On top of it, she could bake. One evening, Pam brought a cherry pie for dessert, which I assumed was from a mix or had been purchased. She actually made it from scratch, and it was the best that I had ever tasted.

I grew up with dogs, but Pam was a cat lover and convinced me to adopt a kitten. I chose a six-week-old orange tabby from an animal shelter that I named Rico, the acronym for the Racketeer Influenced and Corrupt Organizations Act under which I prosecuted individuals. He turned out to be a great wingman as Pam began to spend more time at my place visiting him, and I too became a beneficiary of the increased visits.

After a year together, it seemed like a good time to think about marriage. We had dinner and watched a show at Blues Alley in Georgetown on a Saturday evening. That night, we stayed downtown at the Grand Hyatt Washington, which was where I proposed to her. The next day, we went to a jeweler, who had the ring that I had already chosen for her. She loved it, and we were officially engaged. We got married on May 2, 1992, a few weeks from Pam's thirtieth birthday, at Montpelier Mansion in Laurel, Maryland, a plantation house that George Washington had once used while traveling. Nan and her husband, Judge Robert Shuker, jointly officiated the wedding.

The honeymoon started off with a bang. Our plan was to fly to Las Vegas via Los Angeles, spend a night there, and then rent a car to go to the Grand Canyon. However, we were traveling to LA right after the police officers had been acquitted in the Rodney King case. Due to the rioting, our original flight was cancelled, but the airline was able to put us on another one. As we approached Los Angeles International Airport, things became intense because some of the rioters were firing guns at incoming planes. We ended up circling in the air for an hour before our plane received the green light to land as a result. Pam and I were exhausted and irritable, which was not a good start. When we picked up the rental car, the honeymoon officially began. After a pleasant drive, we reached the Grand Canyon. Once we saw the steepness of the trail and the size of the mules, we opted for a smooth river excursion instead, and all was swell.

After a couple of years, we wanted a family. There was never a question of how we would do it. I contacted a social worker whom I had known through the DC Child and Family Services Agency. She now worked for the Jewish Social Service Agency, a private organization. While in the process of adopting a baby in Indiana, she learned that Nicholas, a biracial infant who was born on May 13, 1995, was available. Two and a half months later, we flew to Louisville, Kentucky, with a car seat. The next day, we drove one hour to Evansville, Indiana, where the adoption agency was located, to meet Nicholas, his birth mother, and foster family.

Nicholas's birth mother was a nineteen-year-old woman who did not want her son growing up under the influence of her mother, so she put him up for adoption. After spending some time with her, Pam and I left the mother to go to another room, where she presented Nicholas to us. I will never forget the moment when he was handed to me. He was a calm, happy, and responsive baby. He was perfect.

Much to our surprise, the agency told us that we could take Nicholas home for the night after we met with the adoption attorney, so we drove back to our hotel in Louisville with our new son. Since we had no idea what to do with him, we called Pam's mother in Minnesota. She suggested that we ask the hotel for a crib, and our first night as a family began. The next morning, we made our way back to Evansville to visit his foster family and retrieve his belongings. While there, we received more unexpected news. The Interstate Compact on the Placement of Children, which allowed us to bring Nicholas back with us from Indiana back to DC, was already signed. We dressed him in a Baltimore Orioles jumper that we had brought with us, said our goodbyes, and headed back to Louisville for the flight home. I called my parents, and they were at the airport when we arrived with their new grandson.

We kept in touch with Nicholas's biological mother through letters via the adoption agency. They called us two years later to let us know that a biracial baby girl was available in Indiana. We were not ready for a second child, but when they sent us a photograph of her, we warmed up to the idea and asked the Lutheran Social Services in DC to conduct a home study. During this period, she was no longer available because members of her biological family had been located. We were very disappointed because we now liked the idea of having a daughter. The social worker that had prepared our home study for the Indiana baby informed us that there was a biracial baby girl available in DC. We jumped at the opportunity. Rachel was born on February 9, 1997, and we brought her home six weeks later.

Since Nicholas had been such an easy-going baby, it would only make sense that we would have to pay our dues. Rachel was a crying machine. She was stubborn and a drama queen when she did not get her way. "That's a willful child!" my mother would say. Eventually, she developed a lighter side, always singing and dancing. I called her my princess and used to sing to her that she must have been a beautiful baby to be such a beautiful girl.

CHAPTER 6

On November 4, 1992, Judge Webber, a long-standing friend of my father, swore me in as an associate judge of the Superior Court of the District of Columbia. Pam held the Bible, my parents robed me, and everyone in my family, even Pam's mother, was in attendance. It was especially significant for me because the chief judge that had presided over my investiture was Frederick Ugast, who was practically a member of the family. He had been my father's supervisor when they worked together at the Department of Justice. I had known him since I was thirteen years old. His son Tommy was in my high school graduating class, and his other son Fred was in my brother's. The Satterfield and Ugast brothers and our fathers had a special shared memory; we had attended the Washington Senators' final game at RFK Stadium on September 30, 1971, before the team moved to Texas.

The link to my father was important because my father had motivated me to do many things in life. He helped me overcome cancer, my disability, and my divorce. He also inspired me to become a judge.

My family always called me Little Lee, which is ironic because I turned out to be a good deal taller than my father, who was always referred to as Big Lee. I was proud to be named after him, but the expectations were high, especially after I entered the same profession. He had always wanted to be a judge, but had put his dream aside to care for me. When he obtained another application years later, he gave it to me instead. "You should be a judge," he told me. "You can do more for our community as a judge than you're doing as an attorney."

Over the next few days, I filed my application with the DC Judicial Nomination Commission. It consisted of one member appointed by the chief judge of the United States District Court for the District of Columbia, the US president, and chairman of the DC City Council, and two members appointed by the DC Bar, the and the DC mayor. The commission interviewed me, and on that same day, I received a call from the chair informing me that my name was one of three being sent to President George H. W. Bush. After all of us were interviewed by the White House Counsel's Office, Brook Hedge, another Justice Department attorney and I were nominated to fill the two vacancies. After testifying at a Senate committee hearing, we were both confirmed.

Assuming the mantle of a judge was a challenge. Despite my many years as a prosecutor, I was filled with anxieties at the start. I learned that other judges had also felt the same insecurities in their first days. My judicial career began with misdemeanor cases like drug possession and shoplifting. One of them involved a motion to suppress evidence due to an illegal search. I felt that the police witnesses were not credible, but I knew that if I did not allow the evidence to be admitted, the case would not go forward. I was nervous about taking such a bold step as a neophyte. I remembered that Judge Robert Shuker had offered his help if I needed it. "Just step off the bench and come see me," he had told me. His approach was not what I expected. He never gave me his opinion since he knew that I would simply follow it, and I would have because I was in awe of him. Instead, he made it into a learning experience by asking me several questions regarding the police witnesses. Once I had reached my conclusion, he said, "Okay, I think you're ready to rule." I went back to court and suppressed the evidence.

On June 28, 1993, Shuker died from a heart attack while jogging the C&O Canal towpath. After he passed, Nan took Shuker's surname and became my mentor. She gave me one of her husband's robes, which I proudly wore for many years.

At the end of 1993, Chief Judge Ugast and Judge Frederick Weisberg, who was the presiding judge of the Criminal Division, singled me out for my next assignment as one of three judges asked to manage the first specialty court, the Superior Court Drug Intervention Program, also known as Drug Court. The idea had originated from a group of judges and court administrators in Miami, Florida, where the first drug court began. Based on empirical studies, they agreed that drug addiction was an illness given the many faces repeatedly coming before them on drug possession offenses; therefore, the system could better manage those cases by solving the underlying problem, the individual's drug addiction.

Drug Court was established as a therapeutic alternative, a place where drug-addicted defendants could receive intensive treatment and other services to stay clean. They would be randomly drug tested and monitored by a judge, who would review their progress and either dismiss the case for doing well or sanction them for not living up to their obligations. The DC Superior Court was the second court in the nation to start such a program.

I was initially disappointed with the assignment. I was hoping to move on to something more substantial like serious felony trials, but it turned out to be a terrific opportunity. It opened my eyes to a different aspect of handling recurrent drug offenders. Prior to Drug Court, I used the traditional adversary model: a judge presided over a trial by making evidentiary rulings—rulings on what evidence must or must not be admitted. If a defendant was found guilty after instructing the jury on the law, then the judge would sentence them. Only at that time could they receive treatment for the addiction. In any case, they would still have a criminal conviction on record.

It was rewarding to observe the positive impact this approach had on the defendant, his family, and the community where he lived. I was so inspired by this approach that when I later became presiding judge of Family Court, I helped create a treatment court for drug-addicted mothers whose children were in foster care. Under this program, those children could safely live with their mothers while their addiction was being treated.

In 1997, Chief Judge Eugene Hamilton assigned me to be presiding judge of the Domestic Violence Unit. I met with domestic violence advocates and other stakeholders. I kept seeing victims follow the cycle of domestic violence, either by failing to obtain a protective order against the perpetrator, not cooperating with prosecutors in criminal cases brought against the perpetrator, or, in many cases, going back to the perpetrator. Wanting to get a better understanding of the victim mentality, I attended judicial education programs on domestic violence sponsored by national organizations. I became intrigued with the challenges faced by the victims if they left their abusers. Many risked being killed; others risked falling into poverty and homelessness and possibly losing custody of their children. I was sympathetic to their plight and wanted to figure out ways for them to break the cycle. I took part in additional educational programs, learning in greater detail about the need to educate judges nationwide on the complexities confronting a victim when making the decision to stay with the abuser, the best methods to navigate the complexity of such relationships, and recognizing that the victim's safety was the paramount objective.

When Hamilton resigned as chief judge in 2000, I decided to apply for the position. Six other more senior judges also applied, including the succeeding Chief Judge Rufus King. Although I knew that I was not ready yet, I thought the experience would be beneficial and make people aware that it was a position that I hoped to obtain in the future.

On December 24, 1999, Judge Evelyn Queen returned twenty-three-month-old Brianna, who had been living in foster care, back to the birth mother, Charissa Blackmond, without holding a hearing. From then until January 5, she was repeatedly abused by her godmother, Angela O' Brian, who was living with Blackmond at the time. Brianna died on January 6, 2000. The testimonies of the first responders, the doctors who treated her, the medical examiner, and O'Brian's children established that during the twelve-day period that Brianna was given back to Blackmond, she was handcuffed to a stroller, picked up by her shirt and dropped on her head and face several times, punched in the chest, and whipped with a belt. The autopsy determined that the blunt force trauma resulted in subdural hemorrhages covering much of the surface of her brain and around the optic nerves and retinas, and bleeding in the subarachnoid space.

Brianna's tragic fate struck a chord with many, including congressional leaders like House Majority Leader Tom DeLay and DC representative Eleanor Holmes Norton. As a result, Congress passed the District of Columbia Family Court Act in 2001, overhauling the Family Division of Superior Court and renaming it Family Court. Following the enactment, King asked me to lead the new court as its first-ever presiding judge. This new assignment was largely based on my experience presiding over the Domestic Violence Unit. During the selection process, the commission members told him that they had been impressed by my performance, and he should consider giving me leadership opportunities during his tenure.

Becoming presiding judge of Family Court meant that I would be overseeing twenty judges instead of three. It was a great test of my leadership skills, and in preparation, I read countless books on the subject. Leadership, I decided, meant giving positive direction to an organization, fostering the people within it, and adding value to the community served by the organization. It was important to be fair, supportive, and progressive. Accountability was also critical.

The judges and staff at Family Court were exceptional. They were hardworking and committed to the mission. We held public forums, established goals, and tackled core family issues, such as a child's educational needs or a parent's unemployment. Over the course of four years, we implemented numerous reforms. After reviewing those changes, the Government Accountability Office found that cases of child abuse and neglect were being handled much better and more expeditiously, which translated to children leaving foster care quicker. Howard Davidson, the director of the ABA Center on Children and the Law, said that Family Court had become a model for court agency and community partnership.

As a result of our successes, my colleagues elected me to serve on the court's Joint Committee on Judicial Administration.

In September 2006, I was walking back to the courthouse from lunch when I was overwhelmed by a shortness of breath. I hailed a cab and went to the emergency room at George Washington University Hospital. Fearing I had inherited his heart problems, my father appeared at the hospital with his cardiologist, Dr. Richard Katz. It turned out that my father was off the hook; his DNA was not the cause of my problem. The chemotherapy that had cured my cancer was.

It had taken thirty years for the massive doses of chemo that I had undergone to affect my heart. I was diagnosed with chemotherapy-induced cardiomyopathy, a condition in which the heart muscle is damaged, and as a result, blood is not adequately pumped. Whereas most people cruise on a six-cylinder engine, I now had a four-cylinder that required the right mix of medication in order to get back up to six. I was in the early stages of heart failure.

On October 25, I received a call from Pam right after I had dropped the children off at school. My father had been found unconscious in his car while parked in front of Lori's house and was taken to Walter Reed Army Medical Center. As I headed for the hospital, my gut feeling told me that this was it. His heart had finally stopped. Big Lee was already dead from his third heart attack by the time I arrived. I mourned for the man who had been so central to my life, but I also celebrated his life. He was always optimistic and inspired me to reach for great heights, while wisely guiding me along the way. Although I had just suffered a great loss, I was thankful to have been the recipient of pure fatherly love.

Lee with former Chief Judge Fred Ugast at the Columbus
School of Law of The Catholic University of America.

At a Washington Redskins game with Lee's
father, Lee Arthur Satterfield.

CHAPTER 7

After vying for chief judge in 2000, my interest in the position increased. So when Chief Judge King announced in 2008 that he would not seek a third term, I jumped at the chance. This time around, only one other associate judge applied. A candidate forum was held midsummer, and after we were both interviewed by the commission in August, I received a call from the chair informing me that I was going to be the next chief judge. On September 30, Rufus swore me in before many of the same people who had attended my first investiture. Only one special person was missing—my father; however, I could feel that he was there in spirit.

My role as chief judge was to administer the business of the court. This included caseload division, judge assignments, and budget management. However, the manner in which one manages was not defined. I chose to lead as part of a team and created the Judicial Leadership Team, which consisted of the presiding and deputy presiding judges of each division. I chose this path because of what I had learned working with King, who had delegated significant administrative responsibilities to me as presiding judge of Family Court. This practice was also consistent with what I thought about leadership—the top executive should do what he can do best and assign the remaining tasks to those who can better handle them. It kept everyone engaged and made them a team player. It also demonstrated to them that I trusted and valued their input. Lastly, it allowed me the time to plan for the future and anticipate what would be needed.

I also sought to strengthen the relationship between "the robes and suits"—the judges and division directors who supervised the majority of court staff—and enhance performance, transparency, and accountability through the Chief Judge and Clerk of the Court Performance Standard Team. The team members created case-management plans, which were published on the court's website. They spelled out the best practices that a judge should do to manage a particular case type. Before adopting these plans, each judge managed their caseload as they saw fit, which varied considerably between judges. This resulted in decision-making inconsistencies, missed deadlines, delays, and increased waiting time for all parties involved. It was also the primary reason Congress had passed the Family Court Act and mandated a one judge, one family case-management approach. It taught me that if we did not hold ourselves accountable and manage our cases well, the legislative branch would.

During King's terms, the precursor to the team I created developed performance guidelines that set forth trial date certainty and time-to-disposition standards. I added jury utilization to the mix. The aim was to have 90 percent of the jurors summoned daily to serve. Aside from administration procedures, I concentrated on improving access to justice, which was my way of following my father's insistence that I could do more for the community as a judge than as an attorney. Judges received supplemental training on managing cases involving self-represented parties. I was concerned with tenants settling housing code violations against their landlords; filing a civil action case often took several months to resolve. With the help of Judge Melvin Wright, the presiding judge of the Civil Division, we implemented a housing conditions court, which permitted them to seek expedited relief. The first hearing was scheduled less than a month after the complaint was filed, and the filing fee was a mere fifteen dollars.

I was also interested in reevaluating the effectiveness of some long-standing programs. Juvenile Drug Court was becoming less successful because we were strictly perceiving it as an addiction problem; however, we found that many offenders were abusing substances as a way of dealing with mental health issues. We took a different approach and had many of the offenders participate in a juvenile behavioral diversion program, which was more beneficial to them in the long run. In addition, we expanded the misdemeanor community courts to geographically represent each police district. The focus of these court calendars was similar to those of drug court, which was to determine the underlying cause of an individual's criminal behavior and provide more diversion opportunities for first-time offenders while also holding them accountable by requiring them to complete community service in the neighborhood where the offense took place. They were connected to community resources through city agencies, such as the Department of Employment Services. The objective was to keep them from being saddled with criminal records that could prohibit future employment and reduce the chances of reoffending.

Few couples had as intertwined careers as Pam and I. While our professional lives were progressing smoothly, we were also raising our children as they developed from infants to preschoolers to preteens. When they were young, we took them to Bethany Beach in Delaware for many summers. Once they were able to participate in activities, we sent them to NorthBay Aventure Camp. One summer, Pam and I drove two hours to drop Rachel off in North East, Maryland, only to return home to a phone call from the camp informing us that Rachel had fractured her arm and been taken to a hospital. Apparently, she and her cabinmates were playing bunk bed tag.

Nicholas and Rachel also attended Camp Arena Stage on the Georgetown Visitation Preparatory School campus. Rachel enrolled in dance and theater classes, while Nicholas took music classes. We were so proud to see him as the featured percussionist at the camp's final show. They were both creative and were accepted to the Duke Ellington School of the Arts, but instead chose to attend the school I had gone to—Saint John's College High School. Our last family vacation was to Jackson Hole, Wyoming, in August 2011. We toured the Grand Tetons and Yellowstone. The wildlife in those national parks was amazing. After the trip, we purchased a property east of the Chesapeake Bay Bridge in Grasonville, Maryland. We referred to it as "our bay house," and life was very good in the fall of 2011. Pam and I loved our work. The children were thriving, and we were happy. None of us realized that things were about to change.

Photograph taken after Lee's leadership celebration and Chief Judge Robert Morin's investiture, center. With former Chief Judge Rufus King.

CHAPTER 8

In December of 2008, Dr. Katz recommended an implantable cardioverter-defibrillator to protect me against fatal ventricular tachycardia, a rapid heart rate that could lead to cardiac arrest. As it turned out, his decision was life-saving.

I was giving a speech at a colleague's retirement party in September 2011 when I suddenly felt faint. I stopped speaking and moved toward a chair to sit down, but before I could, I felt a powerful thump in my chest. The impact was so powerful that it knocked me down. My defibrillator had fired for the first time. I realized what had happened, as I was lying there, waiting for my breathing to go back to normal. Eric Washington, the chief judge of the District of Columbia Court of Appeals, was the first person to reach me. Until that moment, no one at the court other than Judge Russell Canan, the presiding judge of the Criminal Division and whom I designated as my fill-in when I was hospitalized for the implant surgery, was aware of my cardiac diagnosis. I was able to stand up and walk out of the room into another judge's chamber, but was taken to the hospital nonetheless. From that moment on, fear that it might happen again accompanied me every time I spoke publicly. In fact, at my first speaking engagement after that incident, I was too anxious to speak. When I arrived at the Washington Convention Center to give welcoming remarks at the Criminal Division's annual training conference, Canan noticed my apprehension and suggested that I return to the courthouse and he would greet the attendees on my behalf. Although I took his advice, I knew that I had to overcome this paralyzing anxiety since public speaking was an essential part of my role as chief judge.

Luckily, the defibrillator delivered a shock only one other time while I was speaking about a year later. Washington and I were scheduled to talk at a luncheon for the DC Bar Board of Governors. Customarily, Washington always spoke first. When he finished, I began speaking when it fired. Washington instantaneously knew what had occurred and took over for me until the brief trauma of the impact wore off. Once I signaled to him that I was okay, he gave the floor back to me. He was a great communicator and was always a friend first.

On November 28, I woke up with a headache and to a full schedule. I assumed the two might have had something to do with each other. The first item on my agenda was to take my mother to her cardiologist appointment. The second item was to attend a funeral service for former chief judge Hamilton. On the way, I checked my work phone and learned that the security officers were concerned that a car parked in front of the main building at the DC courthouse might contain a bomb. I was so preoccupied by the developments at the courthouse that it was not until I arrived at the funeral service that I discovered that I was expected to deliver the eulogy. Another judge had originally agreed to give it; however, since the program listed my name instead, we concluded that this was what Hamilton's family had wanted. Since I was unprepared, I told the pastor about my predicament and asked him to help by adding a spiritual part to it. As I sat in the church waiting for my time to speak, my headache grew more pronounced.

As I headed to the courthouse after the service, I was informed that the possible bomb was a false alarm. I was relieved, but the headache was becoming more and more consuming. Figuring that it was due to not having eaten, I stopped by a McDonald's. When walking to and from the restaurant, I noticed that the left side of my body felt different. When I returned to work, I attended a performance-standards meeting that had been scheduled in my chambers. I wanted it to end because my headache continued to grow stronger. Once it was finished, I went to Special Counsel Rainey Brandt's office to talk to her about the funeral service, which she had also attended. As we were conversing, I thought I was speaking normally, but she noted that I was slurring my words and looked odd, almost sleepy, and my face was droopy. Also, my speech and facial movements were not in sync.

"Chief? Chief? Are you all right?" she asked.

I told her I was fine; I certainly thought so anyway. I just had a headache and an odd sensation—a kind of numbness—on the left side of my body. I said that I only needed to lie down, so I got up and headed to my chambers. However, Brandt had learned the signs of a stroke when she was a Girl Scout.

"No, don't lie down," she said while following me. "You need to just sit. There's something wrong!"

"Nonsense!" I said as I walked into my office and proceeded to lie down on the couch.

"Don't close your eyes! You need to stay awake!"

"C'mon, Rainey. Leave me alone."

"Call 911!" I heard her yell to Christine Maccy, my law clerk. "Tell them it's a possible stroke! And call his wife!"

"No need to call 911," I protested.

Brandt then called Canan. When he laid eyes on me, he immediately yelled, "Call 911!" However, my staff had already done so despite my objections.

Pam, who was working at a law firm three blocks away, arrived at the same time as the EMTs. She climbed into the ambulance, and we headed to George Washington University Hospital. In the emergency room, a doctor began to give me a series of neurological tests. "Raise your arm," she instructed. I could not raise my left arm or see properly out of my left eye and began to have even greater problems speaking. Wanting to confirm a stroke diagnosis, she ordered a CT scan. It showed an arterial blood clot on the right side of my brain. The doctor determined that I was still within the time frame in which tissue plasminogen activator, or tPA, could work. This drug, given intravenously, can dissolve blood clots, resulting in improved blood flow to the part of the brain being deprived of oxygen. By this time, Canan had joined us in the room, and we both started chanting, "Let's bust the clot!"

Our optimism soon waned when there was no dramatic improvement. My symptoms did not begin to lessen after a reasonable period of time; I still could not lift up my left arm. Dr. Wayne Olan, a neurosurgeon, chose to perform a mechanical embolectomy. The procedure consisted of a microcatheter inserted into my groin and threading it through the blocked artery with a clot extractor attached. I was sedated, yet conscious enough to hear the surgeons talk about reaching the clot. Once the tPA was administered, the clot retrieved. The surgeon asked me to lift my left arm, and up it went. Talk about miracles!

Although my left arm was now working just fine, my left hand was not. My speech was no longer affected, and I did not lose any cognitive ability. I was ordered to lie flat in the intensive care unit (ICU) for the next forty-eight hours, the critical period after having a stroke. Every four hours, a nurse came into the room and asked me where I was, the date, and who was president of the United States. I nailed it each time. She also conducted a series of tests, checking the strength of my arms, right leg, and left stump. All were working well, except for my left hand. After ICU, I was moved to the Stroke Treatment Center, where I stayed for ten days.

Because of the excellent care that I received, I was able to walk out of the hospital with no cognitive impairment, only a slight weakness in my left hand, and a prognosis for a full recovery. In addition to the highly-skilled doctors, the rest of the staff, from the housekeepers to the technicians to the nurses, were kind and always smiling, which lifted my spirits at such a critical time. I was so inspired by them that at my first public appearance since the stroke at a work holiday party, I presented a new slogan for the court: More Smiling, Less Complaining.

A couple of months after the stroke, I began to develop pain on the right side of my body. Over the next year, I had numerous tests (ultrasounds, CT scans, endoscopies) with numerous specialists (internists, gastroenterologists, cardiologists), but no one could figure out what was causing the pain. I tried a pain specialist who prescribed Lyrica, a drug for neuropathic pain. I even went the holistic route and saw nutritionists and acupuncturists, but nothing helped.

I was grateful that the tests had not revealed anything fatal, but the pain persisted. By 2013, my appetite had declined, and I had lost more than fifty pounds. I had become dependent on Ambien, a sedative, to overcome the pain so I could fall asleep. In the mornings, I would take Lyrica and suffer blurred vision while driving to work. As my energy levels decreased, my family and colleagues became more concerned, and I began feeling as if I did have a deadly disease. My skin had turned ashen, my body had deteriorated, and my mind had weakened.

The one positive thing that emerged from that dreadful year was that the people of Superior Court turned into a caring family when help was needed. Dinners cooked by an army of judges began materializing at our home, thanks to Judge Zoe Bush, the organizer. Judge Robert Richter's beef brisket and Judge William Nooter's vegan chocolate cake were among the family favorites. Unfortunately, while the thoughtfulness of my coworkers cheered me up, it was not enough to nurse me back to health. One June morning, Pam called me at home since I did not feel strong enough to go to work. She had expressed her fear that I was slowly dying to Dr. Katz, who had suggested that I come to his office. When she told him that I was in no shape for a mere office visit, he agreed to see me at GW Hospital.

I was admitted and underwent more tests, including an echocardiogram. The diagnosis was advanced heart failure. A heart failure specialist from Inova Fairfax Hospital, Dr. Gurusher Panjrath, was advising Dr. Katz, and referred me to the Inova Heart and Vascular Institute, where I went to my initial appointment a few days after discharge. At our first meeting, Dr. Shashank Desai, the medical director of the heart failure and transplant program, said, "Judge, your reputation preceded you, but so did your echo, and you are very sick." It turned out that the pain was being caused by liver congestion. My heart was insufficiently pumping, which resulted in toxins backing up in the liver, unable to be removed. Although this was not an ideal diagnosis, I was relieved. I finally had an answer to the yearlong ordeal.

Something had to be done quickly, so the doctors recommended the implantation of a left-ventricle assistance device, often referred to as a LVAD, a mechanical pump that is attached to the heart and helps pump more blood by continuously taking blood from the left ventricle and moving it to the aorta. They told me it was only a matter of time before the damage to my heart would make it beyond any repair, and if nothing was done, there was only a 50 percent chance that I would survive through the end of the year. I asked Judge Weisberg to take over for me, and on July 2, I checked myself into the hospital for a temporary lease on life.

Lee with Chief Judge Eric Washington at the
Employee Recognition Ceremony in September 2011.
His cardioverter-defibrillator would fire for the first time two weeks later.

CHAPTER 9

By the time I had the LVAD implantation, I was already very sick and weak. When it was over, my surgeon, Dr. Linda Bogar, went to Pam and Lawrence and simply said, "He needed that." I survived the operation but barely made it through postoperative recovery. The right ventricle was not adequately responding to the increased blood flow caused by the pump In an effort to temporarily relieve pressure from the right ventricle, I was intubated for ten days. The drugs that they gave me during my stay induced nightmares. I dreamed that there was a heart available, but that they would not let me have it. I called the court's US marshal, Michael Hughes, to help me, so he sent a deputy to pick me up from our Chesapeake Bay house and transport me to Inova Fairfax Hospital in time to get the heart. In actuality, I was already there. I was so delusional that I fully believed my dreams when I woke up. In one of them, Keith Alexander, a reporter for the Washington Post, which covers DC Superior Court cases, was trying to see me, and that he, in fact, got into my room. I was so convincing that the hospital issued a notice barring Alexander from entry. There was one bright spot amidst the delirium. I thought that I had purchased a beautiful cherry-red Volkswagen Beetle convertible.

Once I was able to breathe on my own, they removed the tube. I awoke to discover that my body had atrophied. I could not move, sit up, or eat without assistance. On top of that, I was still occasionally delusional. I had gotten so frustrated at one point that I told Pam I was taking her out of my will. I also told my mother and Lori that I was going to leave the family when I got out of the hospital. I kept saying awful things and then apologizing afterward.

After the hospital, I went to MedStar National Rehabilitation Hospital for three weeks. Once I was settled at home, I leased the Volkswagen Beetle that I had dreamed about and drove it to work three months after the surgery. Ever the slogan man, I came up with a new one: "Live life with hope, strength, and courage."

Raising teenagers is no easy feat, but when I was not feeling well, it was even more challenging.

During the year and a half prior to the implant, I was in constant pain and felt weak, which in turn made me irritable. The father that my son and daughter had known was no longer there, and their mother was distraught. The happy family of four that they had taken for granted seemed to be falling apart, and at a very vulnerable time for the both of them.

Their frustration with me was apparent. I thought they were selfish and lacked compassion; I expected more from them. After all, I dealt with a significant health challenge when I was their age. Regardless, dealing with your own health challenge as a teenager as opposed to your parent's is very different. "You're faking it, Dad," Rachel remarked when I tried to be upbeat. As she watched me decline and become very fragile, she thought I was going to die. "Dad," she said, "you look like Rico."

Although I had adopted Rico back when Pam and I were dating, he managed to be part of the Satterfield family for many years. However, he was extremely frail right before he died. I told Rachel that I was in good hands because my doctor had been her grandfather's doctor. "Yeah, Dad," she said. "Did you forget that Granddad is dead?"

I later learned that her caustic attitude was a defense mechanism for the devastation she felt. She binge drank to alleviate her emotional state, but came to the conclusion that this was a temporary escape and only made matters worse in the long run. Her psychologist and a former babysitter were finally able to convince her to stop. On the other hand, Nicholas never talked about my health. He later admitted that as he watched me become a different person after the stroke, he did not think he could handle it. He did his best to avoid what was going on at home. During the week, he stayed in his room; and on the weekends, he sought refuge at his friends' houses. He figured that if I had been able to avoid dying from cancer, I would be able to avoid this hurdle too.

He wrote me a letter the Father's Day before the LVAD was implanted:

> Happy Father's Day. You have been through a lot, but you've always been able to get through it. I know in my heart you will be able to heal from what has happened. Again, Happy Father's Day. I love you. Nick

The letter was a boost going into surgery. Unfortunately, the summer that I spent in the hospital affected him significantly. He started drinking and smoking a lot of marijuana. When I came home, I did not recognize him. I did not know how much the situation affected him, but I did notice a lack of motivation during his senior year in high school.

Nicholas was arrested for unlawful entry during the summer of 2014. He got into a neighbor's house through an unlocked back door, mistakenly thinking that it was our house. This was the first indication that he was using K2, a synthetic cannabinoid. Ironically, the community court, which I had expanded across all police districts, helped him out. He completed his community service and was not prosecuted.

Illness put undue pressure on our marriage. I was no longer able to be the person that I once was, and Pam, who used to have her own identity and interests, became my caretaker, which took an enormous amount of her time and energy. This, coupled with other upsetting events in her life, such as a denied judgeship and her father's death, culminated in a great deal of anger and resentment. Our partnership, which had been unbreakable for so many years, began deteriorating. All sexual activity between us ceased.

During Thanksgiving, Pam decided to visit her friend, Gina Abercrombie-Winstanley, the US ambassador to Malta. From the pictures she shared, it seemed like she was relaxed and having a splendid time; but when she returned, things got more intense. I asked her if she still wanted to be married to me. She answered no, and she had planned on telling me when Rachel left for college next fall. She explained that she could not wait for me to get a heart. If I did not get one in time, no one would want her because she would be too old.

On my fifty-sixth birthday, I was not feeling well. Pam no longer wanted to be with me. Nicholas was recovering from substance abuse, and Rachel was emotionally distraught. It was also the second year in a row in which my family forgot about my birthday. I went to work, but I was so upset that I left at noon and drove to our bay house. As I entered the house, I began to fall. Trying to protect the LVAD from damage, I wrapped my arms around it. By doing so, I was unable to break the fall and immediately knew that my left leg did not feel right.

I managed to get up, go to the car, and drive back to Washington. By the time I arrived, I could not get out of the car without the help of the neighbors due to the pain and swelling. After putting down the convertible top, the two of them lifted me up and carried me into the house. For the next three days, I was bedridden in excruciating pain while my defibrillator fired a couple of times. I eventually gave in and went to MedStar Washington Hospital Center, where an X-ray revealed a bone fracture at the hip.

From Christmas to New Year's Day, I was in and out of hospitals, missing out on a family trip to New York. For the first time, I could not use my prosthetic leg. I had to use a wheelchair or a walker to get around. I became even more dependent on my family, which did not make any of us happy. Anxiety, fear, and insecurity had pervaded our relationships. In March of 2015, I decided to move out of the house and lease a one-bedroom apartment on the U Street Corridor. I was fed up with my family since they only saw me as a burden. I wanted to prove to them that I did not need them to survive. However, if I was not going to make it, I preferred to die alone.

On the Friday before Labor Day, I decided to work out at the fitness center. Once I returned to the apartment, I settled down on the couch to watch TV. Several minutes later, my defibrillator delivered a shock. I thought I was okay, but I still called Pam to inform her. Then it fired again and again and again—ten times in ten minutes. I was still on the line with Pam, so she knew exactly what was going on and called 911. I was transported to Washington Hospital Center, where I was stabilized, and then moved to Fairfax Hospital.

I had suffered a VT storm, which is defined as three or more sustained episodes of ventricular tachycardia within a twenty-four-hour period. The following morning, I endured another storm. My medication was adjusted, and I was eventually discharged, but as a result of my rapidly advancing congestive heart failure, I was moved up to the highest category on the transplant list—1A. I started weekly clinic visits until the doctors decided that I had to be hospitalized in order to intravenously receive milrinone, a drug to support my right ventricle. They told me that I would likely remain in the hospital until either the drug stopped working or a heart was available.

On October 28, 2015, I packed a hospital bag, said my goodbyes to Flynn, my cat that I had adopted five months prior, and took a cab to the courthouse. I received a call in the early afternoon that a bed was available. Pam picked me up and drove me to Fairfax Hospital. Once I was settled in, she went home. Later that evening, a nurse came into the room with a cell phone and told me that one of my doctors, Palak Shah, wanted to speak to me. I took the phone, and Dr. Shah asked me how I was doing. He then said the words that I had been waiting to hear for two and a half years, "We have a heart for you." Tears started streaming down my face. The tremendous gratitude and relief that I felt was overwhelming. However, once the doctor began to disclose the required Centers for Disease Control and Prevention information regarding the donor, I snapped back into reality. I had to be immediately brought down to ICU to prepare for the surgery, which was scheduled for early morning. The third-floor nurses gathered my things, put me in a wheelchair, and started pushing me out of the room. As we left, the other nurses were cheering and wishing me good luck. When I reached ICU, I met the nurse in charge of getting me ready for the operation, which took three hours. I was impressed with her style. "You look like you've been through a few of these rodeos," I told her. She acknowledged that she had and continued barking orders. When all was done, she said, "You can sleep now."

In the morning, I was told that the surgery had been bumped to 1:00 p.m. due to logistics at the hospital where the donor was located. At 12:45 p.m., several people in scrubs appeared at my door. One of the nurses began pushing me down the corridor to the operating room and told me that she was going to cry. "Me too," I said.

Recovering from LVAD implantation at MedStar National Rehabilitation Hospital in August 2013 with Nicholas and Rachel.

Lee's first day back at work after LVAD surgery. Judges
Stephanie Duncan Peters and Melvin Wright pictured.

Chapter 10

Recovery was swift. I felt sore but great. For the first time in over a year, I was able to walk and talk at the same time. In fact, I was now talking so much that the nurses called me a chatterbox. I was soon moved out of ICU and back to the third floor. One day, I bumped into my LVAD coordinator. "Hey, Maria," I said, "I got a new heart!"

"I know," she replied, "and not a minute too soon!"

My most triumphant moment was when the nurses permitted me to take a shower. The worst part of the two and a half years with the LVAD was not being able to fully bathe; I had to use the sink to wash myself instead. Although I had a bag to protect the pump from water, I did not want to further jeopardize it since I had only one leg, which increased my risk of falling.

The beginning of my hospital stay was focused on regaining strength, which consisted of daily walks around the ward with a physical therapist. The rest was dedicated to educating me on post-surgery care. For the next few months, my apartment had to be sterile; I was to remain there except for my appointments at the transplant clinic. After a biopsy showed no signs of rejection, I was discharged just two weeks after the surgery on Veterans Day. Pam and Nicholas drove me to my sterile sanctuary, otherwise known as my apartment, and set me up with food. Nicholas helped out with groceries weekly, while Rachel came by for lunch periodically.

I did everything that my transplant team instructed me to do. On Tuesdays, I went to the clinic for blood work and meetings with Mary Beth Maydosz, my transplant coordinator. Every two weeks, a biopsy was performed using a procedure called right heart catheterization, which allows access to the heart via the femoral vein. Fortunately, every biopsy showed no signs of rejection. I kept feeling better and better. In fact, I was recovering so well that I was granted permission to return to work two weeks early on the condition that I would complete a three-month physical cardiac rehabilitation program.

I went back to work on January 19, 2016, with a new slogan: The Beat Goes On. During lunch, I met with Judge Weisberg to recognize his work as acting chief judge during my absence, and the leadership team to thank them for their cooperation with Weisberg. Everyone seemed happy about my return.

In February, I began the rehabilitation program at Inova Alexandria Hospital. I had an hour-and-a-half session three days a week, which included riding a stationary bike, walking on a treadmill, using a cross-trainer, and lifting light weights, all while wearing a heart monitor. Working alongside other cardiac patients and a personal trainer reminded me of my track days. It was very helpful in teaching me about my new physical capabilities. After completing this phase of rehab, I only had to go to the clinic once a month. Everything was improving beyond my imagination.

Before the heart transplant, I did not think that I would survive to the end of my second term as chief judge. After easily completing rehab, I thought about seeking a third term. Since my second term was marred by illness, I felt like there was still work that I wanted to accomplish. However, the support I originally had changed. While the court's services did not suffer, my relationships with some of my colleagues did. They thought I was abrasive and retaliatory, and the newer judges feared me. During my second term, I had difficulty interacting with coworkers and did not always demonstrate compassionate leadership. The anxiety, fear, and knowledge that my health continued to deteriorate overtook my ability to lead such a large, complex organization. I tried my best to make sound decisions in the best interest of the court and community, but the even-tempered, patient leader that they were accustomed to during my first term was not as present as some would have liked. As a result, five members of the past and present judicial leadership teams decided to seek the chief judge position. This was in contrast to when I sought a second term in which my request was not contested. While some may view the competition as a vote of no confidence, it was actually an indication that the leadership culture in which I created was successful in developing my colleagues, who believed they were ready for the next step.

After a short application review period, I received a call from Judge Emmet Sullivan, the commission chairman, on June 16. He informed me that I would not be redesignated for a third term. I was initially disappointed, but once he told me that Judge Robert Morin was going to succeed me, I was pleased. The announcement was made the next day, and

Morin and I met to start the transition. I proposed that he be sworn in on September 30. However, he wanted to deviate from the traditional public investiture and not only be sworn in by me but also have a celebration of my leadership during my two terms. I immediately accepted his counteroffer, and we agreed to schedule the dual event on October 7.

The community response to my leadership was overwhelmingly positive. After administering the oath to Morin, his first act as chief judge was to recognize the DC mayor Muriel Bowser, who proclaimed October 7 as Lee F. Satterfield Day. DC city council chairman Phil Mendelson followed by summarizing a resolution adopted by the council recognizing my leadership as presiding judge of Family Court and chief judge. Afterward, the DC and Washington Bar Associations presented me with certificates of appreciation. I also received a copy of the congressional record that DC representative Eleanor Holmes Norton made recognizing my leadership.

At the end of the celebration, I thanked many people in the courthouse atrium who helped me along my health journey. I also announced that my heart transplant coordinator had notified me earlier in the day that my one-year biopsy showed no signs of rejection. Receiving and publically reporting the good news was very emotional for me because it is the first significant milestone for heart transplant recipients to aspire to reach. I concluded my remarks by leaving the court with my final thoughts: Cherish the present moment, have greater appreciation for life and good health, and build courage and strength to confront life's challenges.

Lee with Dr. Linda Bogar at Inova Fairfax Hospital on
the day of discharge from the heart transplant.

Christmas Day 2015 with Pam, Nicholas, and Rachel.

Judicial Leadership team, 2016. Judge Frederick
Weisberg seated second from left.

Lee speaking at his leadership celebration. October 7, 2016, was
proclaimed by DC Mayor Muriel Bowers as Lee F. Satterfield Day.

Family and friends in attendance at Lee's leadership celebration.

Last day as chief judge at the grand opening of the Northeast Balance and Restorative Justice Drop-In Center. This facility was designed to offer afterschool services to certain at-risk juveniles.

CHAPTER 11

The American Transplant Foundation reports that only about 2,000 to 2,600 hearts are available each year. The LVAD has helped heart failure patients live longer, serving as a bridge to transplant. As a result, about four thousand people are on the waiting list for a heart transplant on any given day. The number of available hearts each year has remained flat. Around 46 percent of the people on the waiting list have been waiting for a year or more.

I was very fortunate to receive a heart. From the moment I was discharged from the hospital, I hoped to one day meet the family of the donor to express my gratitude and learn about the individual who saved my life. I also wanted them to see the positive impact their donation had made. In August of 2016, I received an email from Kathy Briggs, my transplant social worker. "The donor's parents are interested in meeting you," she wrote.

"Absolutely!" I replied. "I would be happy to meet with them."

I had not been told anything about my donor. This was consistent with the practice to keep the identities of both sides confidential. Like a child who had been adopted, I had a tremendous curiosity to know more. Within a couple of days, I received an email from Maureen Balderston of the Washington Regional Transplant Community. She was the family advocate of the donor's parents and suggested a phone chat. I called her that same day and was told that the donor's name was Christopher Canales, the son of Vince Canales and Robin Bright. His parents lived and worked in the DC metropolitan area and wanted to meet me.

Over the course of a couple of weeks, Balderston and I went back and forth about when and where the meeting would happen. During one of our conversations, she told me that Vince and Robin were out of town because Vince's father was very ill. Although they very much wanted to meet, they had to put it off for a while. We were finally able to get together on November 2 at Balderston's office in Annandale, Virginia. I decided to bring Pam. When we arrived, Balderston came down to get us. She said that Vince and Robin were waiting upstairs, and I should be prepared if one of them asked to hear Christopher's heart.

As we walked down the hallway toward the glass-walled conference room, I could see Vince get up to move toward the door. He met me at the entrance with a smile and a hug, which made me more comfortable. I then entered the room, and Robin and I embraced. She greeted Pam, who was holding the flowers that we had gotten for her. I gave them to Robin and confessed that I did not know what to bring to this type of occasion. We all sat down across from each other at a table.

Robin looked at me closely. "I've seen you before," she said. I told her that I was a judge, and she responded that she was also one in Prince George's County. "Do you know Darlene Soltys?" she asked. In fact, I did; Soltys was a new judge at Superior Court. It turned out that they had been at Soltys' investiture. Robin had seen me walking out among the judges and standing on the podium. They had also seen me being interviewed by News4 anchor Doreen Gentzler about the heart transplant, which had aired in February. However, it was not until I entered the room that she made the connection that I had been the one to receive Christopher's heart.

The conversation then shifted to Christopher. He was born on August 28, 1992. He had passed at the age of twenty-three from an asthma attack. He was an old soul who lived life to the fullest. At 2:00 a.m. on October 27, Vince received a call from Christopher's girlfriend informing him that Christopher was in the hospital. Vince rushed over, but as soon as he saw Christopher, he knew that this was the end. Since Christopher was a registered donor, the staff explained the donation procedure to Vince and Robin, and he was kept alive until his organs could be harvested. On the twenty-ninth, they took him off life support.

An hour and a half quickly flew by. We talked about raising children shared photos', and watched the last rap video Christopher created call Showin Love. It was clear to me that Christopher was an aspiring and talented rapper. The meeting went very well for such an unusual situation, considering the happiness and sadness that a heart transplant brings to those involved. Before we left, Robin and I agreed to keep in touch and work together with the transplant community to encourage organ donation. Our second meeting was at the twenty-fifth anniversary gala of the Minority Organ Tissue Transplant Education Program, where Robin was one of the featured speakers. During her remarks, I learned that it was not only Christopher's heart that had been donated but also his liver, kidneys, and tissue. The third time occurred in my chambers when Gentzler interviewed us about our first meeting, which aired on Thanksgiving Day. During the part that was not televised, Gentzler asked Robin if she wanted to hear Christopher's heart beating inside me. She replied that they had purchased a stethoscope for our initial meeting but forgot to bring it. Doreen responded that she had one, but Robin declined; she felt the experience would have been too emotional, and one more appropriately done in private.

I was asked by Dr. Panjrath to be the featured speaker at the Third Annual Heart Failure, Arrhythmia, and Cardiovascular Symposium, hosted by the George Washington University School of Medicine and Health Sciences. In addition to talking about publically living with heart disease, I took this opportunity to thank the medical profession for fighting for me. I let them know that I viewed the surgical scars that they gave me not as unsightly, but rather as badges of my existence. By participating in such an event, it further made me want to spend more time promoting organ donation. If I could do for others in some small way what Christopher Canales and many others had done for me then the remaining of my life would have a true purpose.

Meeting donor's parents Vincent Canales and Robin Bright.

EPILOGUE

During the 1960s, the five-year survival rate for children afflicted with cancer was less than 5 percent. By the 1980s, the rate had increased to 80 percent. Many people made this possible, including the members of Congress for passing the bill and President Richard Nixon for signing into law the National Cancer Act of 1971, which substantially increased funding for cancer research. Researchers and doctors used the funding to improve the treatment for childhood cancer victims. Their collective efforts further increased the survival rate, as evidenced from the fact that almost 11 percent of the five-year survivors in the 1970s were dead within fifteen years of their diagnoses, a percentage that decreased to 6 percent for those diagnosed in the 1990s.

On December 7, 2016, the Childhood Cancer Survivorship, Treatment, Access, and Research Act (also known as the STAR Act) was introduced in the Senate. If passed and signed into law, this will provide additional funding to advance pediatric cancer research and child-focused cancer treatments, while also improving childhood cancer surveillance and developing more pediatric cancer survivor programs, such as the one created at the University of Texas Health Science Center at San Antonio.

The American Childhood Cancer Organization (ACCO) projects approximately five hundred thousand childhood cancer survivors by 2020. Survivors are often afflicted with a number of subsequent health challenges due to the late effects of their cancer treatments, such as cognitive disabilities, neurological defects, and life-threatening complications due to second cancers and heart disorders.

There is an urgency to protect the survivors of childhood cancer. Please join me in the fight against this deadly disease. I intend to dedicate the rest of my life to helping these survivors. Thank you for the gift of your time and interest in my journey.